JOKE BOO
THE ELDERLY

Copyright © 2023 by Robert Titterington.

All rights reserved.
This book is protected by copyright law. No part of this publication may be reproduced, distributed, or transmitted in any form or by any means, including photocopying, recording, or other electronic or mechanical methods, without the prior written permission of the copyright holder, except in the case of brief quotations embodied in critical reviews and certain other noncommercial uses permitted by copyright law.

The content in this book, including but not limited to jokes, illustrations, and original material, is the intellectual property of the copyright holder and is protected under applicable copyright laws. Any unauthorized use or reproduction of this material may violate copyright laws and result in legal action.

The author and publisher have made every effort to ensure the accuracy of the information presented in this book. However, they make no representations or warranties regarding the completeness, accuracy, reliability, or suitability of the information. The author and publisher shall not be held liable for any errors, omissions, or damages arising out of the use of this book.

Dear reader,

Get ready to laugh, giggle, and chuckle your way through this joy-filled journey. Let these jokes bring a spark of happiness into your life, inspire you to embrace the lighter side of things, and leave you feeling uplifted. Remember, the gift of laughter is meant to be shared, so spread the joy to those around you and make the world a brighter place, one smile at a time.

Let the laughter and inspiration begin!

TABLE OF CONTENTS

CLASSIC JOKES	4
SENIOR MOMENTS	15
FAMILY AND RELATIONSHIPS	25
TECHNOLOGY AND GADGETS	35
AGING AND HEALTH	45
RETIREMENT AND LEISURE	55
WISDOM AND LIFE LESSONS	65
DAILY ROUTINES	75
SENIOR ADVENTURES	85
LAUGHTER THERAPY	95

CLASSIC JOKES

Why don't scientists trust atoms?
Because they make up everything!

• • •

Why did the chicken cross the road?
To get to the other side!

• • •

What do you call a bear with no teeth?
A gummy bear!

• • •

Why don't skeletons fight each other?
They don't have the guts!

• • •

Why couldn't the bicycle find its way home?
It lost its bearings!

•••

What's brown and sticky?
A stick!

•••

What do you call a fish with no eyes?
Fsh!

•••

Why did the scarecrow win an award?
Because he was outstanding in his field!

•••

Why don't eggs tell jokes? Because they might crack up!

• • •

Why was the math book sad?
Because it had too many problems!

• • •

Why don't they play cards in the jungle?
Because there are too many cheetahs!

• • •

What's the best time to go to the dentist?
Tooth-hurty (2:30)!

• • •

Why did the tomato turn red?
Because it saw the salad dressing!

•••

What do you call a fly without wings?
A walk!

•••

Why did the golfer bring two pairs of pants?
In case he got a hole in one!

•••

What do you get when you cross a
snowman and a vampire?
Frostbite!

•••

What do you call a bear with no teeth?
A gummy bear!

•••

Why don't oysters donate to charity?
Because they are shellfish!

•••

What do you call a fake noodle?
An impasta!

•••

What musical genre do seniors with arthritis
listen to?
Pop.

•••

Why don't elephants use computers?
Because they're afraid of the mouse!

•••

What did one wall say to the other wall?
"I'll meet you at the corner!"

•••

What's the best way to communicate with a
fish? Drop them a line!

•••

How do you catch a squirrel?
Climb a tree and act like a nut!

•••

What do you call a deer with no eyes?
No idea!

•••

How do you organize a space party?
You "planet"!

•••

What did one hat say to the other hat?
"You stay here, I'll go on ahead!"

•••

How do you catch a runaway dog? Hide
behind a tree and make a "barking" sound!

•••

What did one elevator say to the other elevator?
"I think I'm coming down with something!"

•••

How do you make a tissue dance?
Put a little boogie in it!

•••

Why don't skeletons play music in church?
Because they have no organs!

•••

Why don't older mermaids like to swim in the ocean?
They're afraid of getting a mammogram!

•••

What do you call bears with no ears?
B–.

•••

What did one hat say to the other hat?
"You stay here, I'll go on ahead!"

•••

What's the difference between a poorly
dressed man on a tricycle and a well-dressed
man on a bicycle? Attire!

•••

Why aren't koalas actual bears?
They don't meet the koalafications.

•••

What did one plate say to the other plate?
"Dinner is on me!"

•••

What's orange and sounds like a parrot?
A carrot!

•••

How does a penguin build its house?
Igloos it together!

•••

How do you make holy water?
You boil the hell out of it!

•••

What do lawyers wear to court?
Lawsuits.

• • •

I told my physical therapist I broke my arm
in two places.
He told me to stop going to those places.

• • •

What do you call someone with no body
and no nose? Nobody knows.

• • •

What did the football coach say to the
broken vending machine?
Give me my quarterback.

• • •

SENIOR MOMENTS

Why did the senior bring a ladder to the bar?
Because they heard the drinks were on the house!

●●●

How do you know when a senior is having a "senior moment"?
When they search for their glasses while wearing them!

●●●

Why did the senior put their phone in the fridge?
They wanted to cool down their "hotline"!

●●●

What did the forgetful senior say when
asked about their age?
"I can't remember, it must have slipped
my mind!"

●●●

Why did the senior take a nap in the library?
They wanted to "read between the snores"!

●●●

How did the senior fix their "senior moment"
of misplacing their glasses?
They found them on top of their head!

●●●

How do you confuse a senior?
Ask them to count backwards from ten,
starting with their age!

●●●

Why did the senior put their TV remote
in the fridge?
They were trying to "cool down"
the TV shows!

•••

What did the senior say when they forgot
their password?
"I must have changed it to something
I can't remember!"

•••

Why did the senior bring a rake to
the beach?
They wanted to "leave their mark"!

•••

How do you make a senior's day?
Bring them a cup of coffee and remind
them where they left it!

•••

Why did the senior put their glasses in the freezer?
They wanted to "cool down" their vision!

●●●

What did the forgetful senior say when they saw a birthday cake?
"I can't remember blowing out so many candles!"

●●●

How do you keep a senior's attention?
Write it down and put it in large font!

●●●

Why did the senior take a ladder to the concert?
They heard it was a "high note" performance!

●●●

How did the forgetful senior describe their favorite movie?
"I can't recall the title, but it had that famous actor... you know, the one with the face!"

•••

What did the senior say when they forgot their own phone number?
"I guess I'll have to call myself to find out!"

•••

Why did the senior wear mismatched shoes?
They couldn't find the other pair, but at least they had a backup!

•••

What did the senior say when they forgot where they parked their car?
"I must have invented a new hide-and-seek game!"

•••

How did the forgetful senior describe their recent vacation?
"It was somewhere with lots of sunshine and palm trees... or was it a postcard I saw?"

•••

Why did the senior bring an empty wallet to the store?
They wanted to test their "window shopping" skills!

•••

How did the senior react when they forgot someone's name?
"I must have left it in my other memory bank!"

•••

Why did the senior wear their reading glasses to the theater?
They wanted to get a "close-up" of the actors!

•••

What did the forgetful senior say when they couldn't find their keys?
"I guess I'll just follow my footsteps to remember where I left them!"

•••

How did the senior describe their search for the TV remote?
"It was like an Olympic event... I went from couch to couch!"

•••

Why did the senior take a selfie with their groceries?
They thought it would help them remember what they needed!

•••

How did the senior react when they forgot the punchline to a joke?
"I guess I'll just have to laugh and pretend I remembered!"

•••

Why did the senior bring a magnifying
glass to the restaurant?
They wanted to read the fine print
on the menu!

●●●

What did the forgetful senior say when they
couldn't find their favorite TV show?
"I guess I'll have to watch the news... again!"

●●●

How did the senior describe their
attempt at multitasking?
"I was trying to remember what I was
doing while doing something else!"

●●●

Why did the senior bring a shopping list
to their own birthday party?
They didn't want to forget what
presents they wanted!

●●●

What did the forgetful senior say when they misplaced their glasses?
"I must have given them a vacation from my nose!"

•••

How did the senior react when they couldn't find their car in a parking lot?
"I think I parked it in the 'hide-and-seek' section!"

•••

Why did the senior bring a calendar to the movie theater?
They wanted to mark the date when they saw the film!

•••

What did the forgetful senior say when they couldn't remember their favorite recipe?
"I'll just have to cook from the heart and hope it turns out!"

•••

How did the senior describe their attempt at using a smartphone?
"It's like a puzzle... I swipe left, swipe right, and hope I end up on the right app!"

●●●

Why did the senior bring a notepad to their own wedding anniversary celebration?
They didn't want to forget all the reasons they fell in love!

●●●

What did the forgetful senior say when they misplaced their shoes?
"I must have given them a break from my feet!"

●●●

How did the senior react when they forgot their own age?
"I'll just celebrate my 'forever young' status!"

●●●

FAMILY & RELATIONSHIPS

Why did the grandma challenge her grandson to a dance-off?
She wanted to prove that her "groovy" moves could still outshine his TikTok videos!

•••

What did the dad say when his child asked why they had so many family traditions? "Well, we have to keep practicing until we perfect them! Plus, it's an excellent excuse for more cake!"

•••

Why did the grandpa start learning magic tricks? He wanted to "pull" some laughter out of his sleeves and leave his grandkids in awe of his magical skills!

•••

What did the mom say when her children
complained about doing household chores?
"Hey, cleaning is a family Olympic sport! Let's see
who can dust the fastest and mop the smoothest!"

●●●

What did the mom say when her child asked why
they always had family movie nights?
"It's our way of preparing for the next family
trivia night—popcorn, laughter, and
some serious note-taking!"

●●●

Why did the family decide to start a tradition of
costume parties?
They wanted to unleash their inner
superheroes, embrace their silly side, and
create unforgettable photo ops!

●●●

Why did the parents decide to take up salsa
dancing?
They wanted to spice up their relationship, heat
up the dance floor, and impress their children
with some killer moves!

●●●

What did the sibling say to the other sibling who always borrowed their clothes?
"Alright, I see what's happening here. It's time to create a fashion contract with severe penalties for unauthorized clothing borrowing!"

●●●

What did the kids say when their parents asked for help with technology?
"Sure, we'll help you. But in exchange, you have to promise not to embarrass us with any more embarrassing baby photos!"

●●●

Why did the family start a tradition of weekly karaoke nights?
To prove that singing in the shower wasn't their only talent and to unleash their inner rock stars!

●●●

What did the mom say when her child asked about the importance of family?
"Honey, family is like a box of chocolates—sometimes sweet, sometimes nutty, but always full of love!"

●●●

Why did the siblings plan a surprise flash mob for their parents' anniversary?
To show that their love was contagious, their dance moves were epic, and their family was full of surprises!

•••

What did the dad say when his children asked why they always had family picnics?
"It's our way of proving that ants aren't the only ones who can have a picnic party—it's time for the humans to join in!"

•••

What did the grandpa say when his grandchild asked about the secret to a happy marriage?
"Oh, it's simple—always let your grandma have the last word, and make sure it's 'I'm sorry, dear!'"

•••

What did the grandparents say when their grandchild asked about the secret to a happy family?
"Well, it involves equal parts of love, laughter, and knowing when to let grandpa win at board games!"

•••

What did the mom say when her child asked why they always had family road trips?
"Well, it's a great way to test our patience, bond over questionable rest stop food, and create memories that GPS can't guide!"

●●●

What did the dad say when his child asked about the secret to a happy marriage?
"Well, I'll let you in on a little secret—always let your mom think she's right, and you'll have a lifetime supply of peace!"

●●●

Why did the grandma start taking karate lessons?
She wanted to show her grandkids that age is just a number and that she could still deliver some "karate-chop" jokes!

●●●

Why did the grandparents start learning magic tricks?
They wanted to prove that they could make wrinkles disappear, laughter appear, and turn grandkids into amazed audience members!

●●●

Why did the family start a tradition of hosting talent shows?
To showcase their hidden talents, compete for the coveted "Family's Got Talent" trophy, and laugh until their sides hurt!

●●●

What did the dad say when his child asked why they always had family game nights?
"Well, it's a great opportunity for me to show off my unbeatable Scrabble skills and teach you some life lessons about strategic wordplay!"

●●●

What did the mom say when her child asked about the importance of family?
"Darling, family is like a human puzzle—each piece fits together perfectly, and when one is missing, the picture just isn't complete!"

●●●

Why did the siblings plan a surprise trip for their parents?
To give them a break from their daily routine, create new memories in a different place, and show their gratitude for all the love and support!

●●●

What did the mom say when her child asked why they always had family movie nights?

"It's the perfect way to avoid spoilers, eat excessive amounts of popcorn, and create epic debates over who should have won the Oscar!"

• • •

Why did the family decide to start a tradition of annual treasure hunts?

To tap into their inner adventurers, solve mind-boggling riddles, and compete for the title of "Family Treasure Hunting Champions!"

• • •

What did the dad say when his child asked why they always had family barbecues?

"Because our grill is the stage, the sausages are the stars, and the backyard is our arena for culinary greatness!"

• • •

Why did the family start a tradition of creating wacky home videos?

To unleash their inner comedians, star in their own hilarious sketches, and create memories that would make them laugh for years to come!

• • •

Why did the siblings challenge their parents to a video game tournament?
They wanted to show that they could still beat them at their own game, both literally and figuratively!

• • •

Why did the siblings organize a surprise flash mob for their parents' anniversary?
They wanted to remind their parents that love can still make them dance like nobody's watching, even after all these years!

• • •

What did the dad say when his child asked why they always had family camping trips?
"Because nothing brings us closer than sharing a tiny tent, battling bugs, and attempting to start a campfire without burning down the forest!"

• • •

Why did the siblings challenge their parents to a cooking competition?
To prove that their family recipes were worthy of Michelin stars and to create a delicious rivalry filled with taste tests and culinary surprises!

• • •

Why did the grandparents start learning salsa dancing?
They wanted to show that love could be as fiery as their dance moves, and they were ready to spice up the family gatherings!

●●●

What did the mom say when her child asked why they always had family picnics?
"Well, darling, nature is our way of reminding ourselves that no Wi-Fi signal is as strong as the connection we share!"

●●●

What did the grandparents say when their grandchild asked about the secret to a happy family?
"Well, darling, it involves equal parts of love, laughter, and knowing when to let grandma win at card games!"

●●●

Why did the parents decide to take up skydiving?
They wanted to experience the ultimate "leap of faith" together and prove that their love could soar to new heights!

●●●

What did the mom say when her child asked why they always had family art projects?
"Because creativity is the glue that holds us together, and the fridge is our gallery showcasing masterpieces that money can't buy!"

●●●

Why did the grandparents start a band?
They wanted to show the world that they still had the rock 'n' roll spirit and that age couldn't stop them from hitting the high notes!

●●●

Why did the family start a tradition of annual costume parties?
To let their imaginations run wild, embrace their alter egos, and create memories that would make them laugh for years to come!

●●●

What did the dad say when his child asked why they always had family game nights?
"Well, it's all part of our secret plan for world domination—starting with Monopoly!"

●●●

TECHNOLOGY & GADGETS

Why did the computer go to the doctor?
Because it had a virus!

•••

How do you fix a broken website?
With a URL-aid kit!

•••

Why did the smartphone go on a diet?
It had too many apps and needed to shed
some weight!

•••

What did the router say to the computer?
"You've got mail!"

•••

Why did the elderly person use an umbrella
with their smartphone?
They wanted to protect it from "cloudy"
weather!

•••

How did the computer catch a cold?
It left its Windows open!

•••

Why did the grandma become a
tech-savvy gamer?
She wanted to "level up" her skills!

•••

What did the elderly person say when they couldn't find their TV remote?
"I guess I'll have to exercise by getting up to change the channel!"

●●●

Why did the computer freeze during its yoga class?
It couldn't find its "Ctrl"!

●●●

How did the grandmother describe her experience with virtual reality?
"It's like being in a whole new world without leaving my rocking chair!"

●●●

What did the computer say to the printer?
"You're always paper-ing me with questions!"

●●●

Why did the senior citizen use a tablet at the dinner table?
They wanted to have a "byte" of their favorite recipe!

●●●

How did the grandmother react to her new smartphone's voice assistant? "I'm not talking to myself; I'm just having a high-tech conversation!"

●●●

Why did the senior use a magnifying glass with their smartphone? They wanted to "zoom in" on the small text!

●●●

How did the senior describe their experience with social media?
"I'm making friends and poking buttons like a pro!"

●●●

Why did the grandpa wear a Fitbit? He wanted to prove that he's the "fit-est" grandparent around!

●●●

What did the senior say when their smartphone battery died?
"Guess I'll have to resort to my good old landline!"

●●●

Why did the grandma have a hard time using the touchscreen?
Her fingers were "too seasoned" for modern technology!

●●●

How did the grandparent describe their video chat experience?
"It's like having a face-to-face conversation without leaving my favorite chair!"

●●●

Why did the senior citizen bring a GPS on their morning walk?
They didn't want to get lost in the neighborhood!

● ● ●

What did the elderly person say when they got a smartwatch?
"Now I have a personal assistant on my wrist!"

● ● ●

How did the grandma describe her experience with voice-activated devices?
"It's like having a personal butler at my command!"

● ● ●

Why did the senior wear noise-canceling headphones?
They wanted to enjoy their favorite music without any distractions!

● ● ●

What did the grandpa say when he learned about wireless charging?
"No more tangled cables for me!"

•••

Why did the senior citizen bring a selfie stick to the family gathering?
They wanted to capture the perfect group photo!

•••

How did the grandma react when she received a new laptop as a gift?
"Now I can surf the internet with lightning speed!"

•••

What did the elderly person say when they learned about 3D printing?
"I can't believe we're living in the future!"

•••

Why did the senior use a password manager? They couldn't remember all their passwords anymore!

●●●

How did the grandparent react to their first experience with virtual reality?
"It's like stepping into a whole

●●●

Why did the senior use a Bluetooth headset? They wanted to have hands-free conversations like a secret agent!

●●●

What did the elderly person say when they discovered emojis? "I never knew a tiny image could express so much!"

●●●

Why did the grandma take a selfie with her tablet?
She wanted to show her friends how she's keeping up with the latest technology trends!

•••

How did the grandpa react to voice recognition technology?
"I can finally have a conversation with my computer without typing a single word!"

•••

What did the senior say when they discovered streaming services?
"Goodbye, VHS tapes! Hello, endless entertainment at my fingertips!"

•••

How did the senior describe their experience with e-books?
"I can carry an entire library in the palm of my hand!"

•••

Why did the grandparent start using a smart thermostat?
They wanted to keep their home cozy without having to get up from their favorite chair!

• • •

How did the grandparent react to facial recognition technology?
"Now my devices recognize me like a long-lost friend!"

• • •

Why did the grandma start using a fitness tracker?
She wanted to make sure she reached her daily step goal and stayed active!

• • •

What did the senior say when they discovered online shopping?
"I can shop for everything I need without leaving the comfort of my home!"

• • •

AGING & HEALTH

Why did the retired doctor become a comedian?
He wanted to keep his patients in stitches!

•••

How do you know you're getting old?
When your back goes out more often than you do!

•••

Why did the senior citizen bring a ladder to the pharmacy?
They heard the prices were "through the roof"!

•••

What did the doctor say to the elderly patient who kept forgetting things?
"I'm sorry, but I can't remember the diagnosis!"

• • •

Why did the senior bring a magnifying glass to the restaurant?
They wanted to "read" the menu!

• • •

How did the elderly person describe their memory?
"It's like a computer with a full hard drive – selective and a bit slow!"

• • •

Why did the senior join a gym?
They wanted to exercise their right to complain about it!

• • •

What did the elderly person say when asked
about their secret to staying healthy?
"Laughter is the best medicine,
followed by naps!"

●●●

Why did the senior citizen take up yoga?
They wanted to improve their flexibility and
become a "bendy" superhero!

●●●

How did the elderly person react when they
found a gray hair?
"I guess it's proof that I'm a silver fox!"

●●●

Why did the retired nurse become a
gardener?
They enjoyed helping plants
"bloom" and grow!

●●●

What did the elderly person say when they couldn't find their glasses?
"I guess I'm just not looking at the bigger picture!"

●●●

Why did the senior bring a tape measure to the doctor's office?
They wanted to measure their height loss!

●●●

How did the grandma describe her age?
"I'm not getting older; I'm just becoming a classic!"

●●●

Why did the senior citizen bring a dictionary to the pharmacy?
They wanted to "pill" up on their vocabulary!

●●●

What did the doctor say to the elderly patient who complained about aches and pains?
"Just remember, you're not old, you're 'well-seasoned'!"

•••

Why did the senior join a dance class?
They wanted to "shuffle" away their worries!

•••

How did the elderly person react when they forgot their own birthday?
"Well, I guess I've reached the age of 'surprise' parties!"

•••

Why did the senior citizen start knitting?
They wanted to "unravel" their stress and create something cozy!

•••

What did the doctor say to the elderly patient who kept losing their keys?
"Perhaps it's time to invest in a key-finding gadget!"

•••

Why did the senior bring a pillow to the doctor's office?
They wanted to be comfortable during the long wait!

•••

How did the grandpa describe his age?
"I'm not old; I'm a vintage edition!"

•••

Why did the retired nurse become a photographer?
They enjoyed capturing the "snapshots" of life!

•••

What did the elderly person say when they couldn't find their glasses again?
"I think they're having a better time without me!"

● ● ●

Why did the senior citizen take up swimming?
They wanted to stay afloat in the sea of aging!

● ● ●

How did the grandparent react when they found a new wrinkle?
"I guess I'm just gaining more character!"

● ● ●

Why did the retired doctor become a chef?
They loved the idea of prescribing delicious meals!

● ● ●

What did the elderly person say when they forgot their own name?
"I guess it's time for a new identity!"

•••

Why did the senior citizen join a choir?
They wanted to exercise their vocal cords and "hit the high notes" of life!

•••

How did the grandparent describe their sleep schedule?
"I have a 'senior siesta' every afternoon!"

•••

Why did the retired nurse become a volunteer?
They wanted to continue caring for others and make a difference!

•••

What did the elderly person say when they couldn't find their hearing aid?
"I guess I'll have to listen extra carefully!"

• • •

Why did the senior citizen start painting?
They wanted to express their creativity and add color to their golden years!

• • •

How did the grandparent react when they found their first gray hair?
"I've earned every silver strand!"

• • •

Why did the retired doctor become a travel enthusiast?
They wanted to explore the world and "doctor" their sense of adventure!

• • •

What did the elderly person say when they couldn't remember their own phone number?
"I think my number got lost in the 'telephone' directory of my mind!"

● ● ●

Why did the senior citizen start writing a memoir?
They wanted to share their wisdom and experiences with future generations!

● ● ●

How did the grandparent describe their sense of humor?
"It's like a fine wine, it gets better with age!"

● ● ●

Why did the retired nurse become a storyteller?
They loved captivating audiences with tales of their colorful career!

● ● ●

RETIREMENT & LEISURE

Why did the retired person take up gardening?
They wanted to prove that they have a green thumb and a golden shovel!

•••

How did the grandparent describe their retirement?
"I'm on permanent vacation mode!"

•••

Why did the senior citizen join a book club?
They wanted to have stimulating conversations and become a literary connoisseur!

•••

What did the retired person say when asked about their daily schedule?
"I have a very important appointment with my recliner every afternoon!"

●●●

Why did the grandma take up painting?
She wanted to create masterpieces and express her artistic side!

●●●

How did the grandpa describe his newfound freedom in retirement?
"I finally have the license to relax and enjoy life!"

●●●

Why did the senior citizen join a dance class after retirement?
They wanted to twirl and waltz their way into a joyful retirement!

●●●

What did the retired person say when asked about their work-life balance?
"Work? I don't know her. Retirement is all about 'play'!"

•••

Why did the grandparent take up birdwatching?
They wanted to observe nature's feathered friends and become a "tweet" expert!

•••

Why did the grandma take up knitting?
She wanted to create cozy masterpieces and keep her loved ones warm!

•••

Why did the senior citizen join a hiking group in retirement?
They wanted to explore nature's wonders and conquer new trails!

•••

How did the retired person react to their first day of retirement?
"I woke up and thought it was the weekend, only to realize every day is a weekend now!"

● ● ●

Why did the senior citizen start writing a memoir in retirement?
They wanted to leave a legacy and share their life's adventures with future generations!

● ● ●

What did the retired person say when asked about their favorite activity?
"Doing nothing and loving every minute of it!"

● ● ●

Why did the grandparent take up fishing in retirement?
They wanted to reel in relaxation and catch some big fish tales!

● ● ●

What did the retired person say when asked about their stress level?
"Stress? That's a word from my past. I'm living a stress-free retirement now!"

•••

What did the retired person say when asked about their retirement plans?
"I plan to have no plans and let spontaneity guide me!"

•••

Why did the grandparent take up photography in retirement?
They wanted to capture the beauty of the world and create lasting memories!

•••

Why did the grandparent take up golf in retirement?
They wanted to perfect their swing and enjoy a leisurely game on the green!

•••

Why did the retiree take up fishing?
They wanted to reel in relaxation and catch some "fin-tastic" memories!

•••

How did the grandparent describe their retirement goals?
"My only goal now is to enjoy life, sip tea, and have endless conversations with friends!"

•••

How did the retired person react when they received their first retirement paycheck?
"Who knew getting paid for not working could feel this good!"

•••

Why did the senior citizen join a cooking class in retirement?
They wanted to become a culinary expert and create delicious masterpieces in the kitchen!

•••

How did the retired person react to their first day of not setting an alarm clock?
"It's pure bliss waking up naturally and letting the day unfold!"

●●●

Why did the senior citizen join a gardening club in retirement?
They wanted to nurture plants and watch their garden bloom with beauty!

●●●

What did the retired person say when asked about their daily commute?
"My commute is now from the bedroom to the living room!"

●●●

Why did the senior citizen join a painting class in retirement?
They wanted to unleash their inner artist and create vibrant works of art!

●●●

Why did the grandparent take up playing musical instruments in retirement?
They wanted to serenade their loved ones with beautiful melodies and harmonies!

•••

How did the retired person react to their first day of retirement travel?
"I felt like a free bird, soaring to new destinations and embracing the world!"

•••

Why did the senior citizen join a writing group in retirement?
They wanted to pen their thoughts, stories, and dreams onto paper and become wordsmiths!

•••

What did the retired person say when asked about their hobbies in retirement?
"I have so many hobbies now that I can't keep track of them all!"

•••

Why did the grandparent take up biking in retirement?
They wanted to feel the wind in their hair and pedal their way to good health!

•••

How did the retired person describe their retirement years?
"It's like being a kid again, but with more experience and wisdom!"

•••

Why did the senior citizen join a theater group in retirement?
They wanted to unleash their inner performer and take center stage in their golden years!

•••

What did the retired person say when asked about their favorite pastime?
"My favorite pastime is simply doing whatever brings me joy in the present!"

•••

Why did the grandparent take up writing poetry in retirement?
They wanted to express their emotions and create lyrical works of art!

●●●

How did the retired person react to their first day of retirement volunteering?
"I realized that giving back is truly fulfilling and brings a sense of purpose!"

●●●

Why did the senior citizen join a language class in retirement?
They wanted to expand their horizons and speak a new language with fluency!

●●●

What did the retired person say when asked about their daily agenda?
"My agenda is open-ended, allowing me to savor life's little pleasures and embrace spontaneity!"

●●●

WISDOM & LIFE LESSONS

Why did the wise retiree always carry a pencil and notepad?
To jot down all the valuable nuggets of wisdom they encountered throughout the day!

●●●

What did the elderly person say when asked about the key to a happy life?
"It's simple: laugh often, love deeply, and always have a stash of chocolate!"

●●●

What did the retired person say when asked about embracing change?
"Life is a constant dance of change. Embrace it, adapt, and find the beauty in every new chapter."

●●●

Why did the wise senior citizen take up mentoring in retirement?
They believed in passing on their wisdom and guiding the next generation towards success!

●●●

What did the retired person say when asked about the secret to a long and fulfilling life?
"Stay curious, keep learning, and never lose your sense of wonder!"

●●●

Why did the grandparent start a book club focused on philosophical works?
They wanted to engage in thought-provoking discussions and ponder the mysteries of life!

●●●

Why did the grandparent take up gardening in retirement?
They understood that nurturing a garden is a metaphor for nurturing oneself and finding peace in the process.

●●●

What did the wise retiree say about the power of perspective?
"It's not what happens to us, but how we perceive and respond to it that shapes our experience and defines us."

●●●

Why did the elderly person start a gratitude practice in retirement?
They recognized that gratitude opens the heart to abundance and shifts focus towards the blessings in life.

●●●

Why did the wise senior citizen take up hiking in retirement?
They believed that nature holds the answers to life's mysteries and offers solace for the soul.

●●●

Why did the grandparent start a gratitude jar in retirement?
They wanted to cultivate an attitude of gratitude by capturing and cherishing the daily moments of joy and appreciation.

●●●

What did the retired person say when asked about the value of friendship?
"True friendships are treasures that enrich our lives, support us in challenging times, and create beautiful memories."

● ● ●

What did the retired person say when asked about the importance of laughter?
"Laughter is the elixir of life. It brings joy, connects hearts, and lightens the heaviest of burdens."

● ● ●

What did the retired person say when asked about the importance of self-reflection? "Self-reflection is the compass that guides us towards self-awareness, growth, and personal transformation."

● ● ●

What did the retired person say when asked about dealing with adversity?
"Life's challenges are like stepping stones that lead us to growth, resilience, and a deeper understanding of ourselves."

● ● ●

Why did the wise senior citizen take up journaling in retirement?
They believed in the therapeutic power of reflection and self-expression in gaining clarity and insight.

● ● ●

What did the retired person say when asked about the value of gratitude?
"Gratitude is the key that unlocks happiness. Count your blessings and watch your life transform."

● ● ●

What did the wise retiree say about the importance of self-care?
"Remember, you can't pour from an empty cup. Prioritize self-care and nurture yourself, body and soul."

● ● ●

Why did the elderly person start volunteering in retirement?
They understood the joy and fulfillment that comes from giving back and making a difference in the lives of others.

● ● ●

What did the wise retiree say about the power of forgiveness?

"Forgiveness is not about condoning the actions of others, but freeing yourself from the burden of resentment."

●●●

Why did the grandparent start practicing mindfulness in retirement?

They recognized that true joy and contentment are found in living fully in the present moment.

●●●

What did the retired person say when asked about their biggest life lesson?

"The best journeys are the ones that lead you to self-discovery and embracing your true authentic self."

●●●

Why did the elderly person take up storytelling in retirement?

They recognized the power of sharing wisdom through stories and passing on lessons to future generations.

●●●

What did the retired person say when asked about the meaning of life?
"Life's true purpose lies in cherishing relationships, finding joy in the simple moments, and leaving a positive impact on others."

●●●

What did the wise retiree say about the importance of self-compassion?
"Be kind to yourself, embrace imperfections, and remember that self-love is the foundation for a fulfilling life."

●●●

Why did the wise senior citizen start a gratitude journal in retirement?
They believed that acknowledging and appreciating the blessings in life amplifies happiness and cultivates a positive mindset.

●●●

What did the retired person say when asked about the importance of self-reflection?
"Self-reflection is the path to self-discovery, growth, and aligning our actions with our true values."

●●●

Why did the grandparent take up meditation in retirement?
They recognized that stillness and inner peace are found in the quiet moments of solitude and self-reflection.

●●●

What did the retired person say when asked about finding purpose in retirement?
"Purpose is not about a grand mission but finding meaning in the small acts of kindness, connection, and contribution."

●●●

Why did the wise senior citizen start practicing gratitude journaling?
They believed that gratitude is the key to unlocking a positive mindset and attracting abundance into one's life.

●●●

Why did the elderly person start practicing gratitude in retirement?
They realized that gratitude is the gateway to contentment and a powerful antidote to negativity and dissatisfaction.

●●●

Why did the elderly person take up meditation in retirement?
They understood the power of stillness and mindfulness in finding inner peace and clarity.

•••

Why did the grandparent take up yoga in retirement?
They recognized the connection between mind, body, and spirit, and the importance of balance in life.

•••

Why did the elderly person take up painting in retirement?
They discovered that art has the power to heal, inspire, and express emotions that words cannot.

•••

What did the retired person say when asked about the importance of lifelong learning?
"The pursuit of knowledge keeps the mind sharp, expands horizons, and fuels a lifelong sense of curiosity and growth."

•••

What did the wise retiree say about the importance of kindness?
"Kindness costs nothing but enriches everyone it touches. Spread it generously!"

• • •

Why did the wise senior citizen start writing their memoirs?
They wanted to share their life experiences, lessons, and triumphs with future generations.

• • •

Why did the wise senior citizen take up gardening in retirement?
They understood that tending to plants mirrors the cycles of life, teaches patience, and allows for connection with nature.

• • •

What did the retired person say when asked about the value of reflection?
"Reflection is the bridge between experience and wisdom. Take time to look back, learn, and grow."

• • •

DAILY ROUTINES

Why did the retiree set three alarm clocks every morning?
They wanted to ensure they had a backup plan in case one clock decided to retire early!

●●●

What did the elderly person say when asked about their morning routine?
"I wake up, stretch my limbs, and count my blessings—starting with how lucky I am to have made it out of bed!"

●●●

Why did the wise senior citizen make their bed every morning?
They believed in starting the day with a small accomplishment and a tidy foundation for success!

●●●

What did the retired person say when asked about their secret to a productive day?
"A strong cup of coffee, a positive mindset, and a to-do list that keeps me on my toes!"

●●●

Why did the grandparent have a strict schedule for breakfast, lunch, and dinner?
They knew that good meals provide nourishment for the body and a reason to gather with loved ones.

●●●

Why did the retiree always take an afternoon nap?
They believed that a short snooze rejuvenates the mind and body, providing an energy boost for the rest of the day!

●●●

What did the wise senior citizen say about the importance of exercise in their daily routine?
"I take a walk every day to keep my joints limber, my heart strong, and my dog happy!"

●●●

Why did the retired person set reminders on their phone throughout the day?
They wanted to stay organized and avoid forgetting important tasks—like where they left their reading glasses!

●●●

What did the grandparent say when asked about their evening routine? "I wind down with a cup of herbal tea, watch my favorite TV show, and cherish the peaceful moments before bedtime."

●●●

Why did the wise retiree always carry a pocket calendar?
They knew that staying organized is the key to a productive day and preventing senior moments!

●●●

What did the elderly person say when asked about their skincare routine?
"I moisturize, use sunscreen, and embrace my wrinkles—they're a roadmap of a life well-lived!"

●●●

Why did the retiree write down their goals for the day every morning?
They believed that setting intentions and having a clear focus increases productivity and satisfaction.

● ● ●

What did the wise senior citizen say about the importance of hydration?
"I start my day with a glass of water and keep a bottle handy—I'm a walking fountain of youth!"

● ● ●

Why did the grandparent always have a crossword puzzle with them during breakfast?
They loved to exercise their brain and sharpen their vocabulary over a bowl of cereal!

● ● ●

What did the retired person say when asked about their evening ritual before bed?
"I brush my teeth, slip into my favorite pajamas, and practice gratitude for another day filled with precious moments."

● ● ●

Why did the elderly person dedicate time each morning to meditation or prayer?
They believed in starting the day with a peaceful mind and setting positive intentions for the hours ahead.

●●●

What did the wise retiree say about the importance of a morning stretch routine?
"I stretch like a cat to keep my body supple and agile—age is just a number, after all!"

●●●

Why did the retiree always have a crossword puzzle book on the coffee table?
They enjoyed challenging their mind, exercising their vocabulary, and having a mental workout at any time of the day.

●●●

What did the grandparent say when asked about their evening routine?
"I sip a cup of chamomile tea, take a leisurely walk around the neighborhood, and enjoy the beauty of the setting sun."

●●●

Why did the wise senior citizen allocate time each day for hobbies and passions?
They believed that pursuing interests keeps the mind engaged, sparks joy, and adds zest to life.

● ● ●

What did the retired person say when asked about their morning ritual?
"I greet the sun with a smile, stretch my body with gentle yoga poses, and thank the universe for another day of possibilities!"

● ● ●

Why did the elderly person have a designated spot for their reading glasses?
They didn't want to waste precious minutes searching for them—time is too valuable for such shenanigans!

● ● ●

What did the wise retiree say about the importance of a morning cup of tea?
"Tea is my daily elixir—it warms my soul, soothes my spirit, and fuels my adventures!"

● ● ●

Why did the retiree have a favorite chair where they would enjoy their morning newspaper?
It was the perfect spot to catch up on the world's happenings and sip a cup of steaming coffee!

●●●

What did the grandparent say when asked about their evening routine?
"I love to indulge in a little dessert before bed— it's the sweet reward for a day well-lived!"

●●●

Why did the wise senior citizen practice deep breathing exercises every day?
They understood that oxygen is life's fuel, and taking mindful breaths brings a sense of calm and clarity.

●●●

What did the retired person say when asked about their morning routine?
"I embrace the beauty of nature with a stroll in the garden—it's a gentle reminder of life's wonders!"

●●●

Why did the elderly person enjoy a leisurely breakfast with their favorite newspaper or book?
They believed in starting the day with a moment of tranquility and mental stimulation.

● ● ●

What did the wise retiree say about the importance of a morning ritual?
"Rituals ground us, provide a sense of stability, and set the tone for a purposeful and fulfilling day."

● ● ●

Why did the retiree always keep a notepad and pen on their bedside table?
They knew that inspiration can strike at any moment, and they didn't want to lose any brilliant ideas!

● ● ●

What did the grandparent say when asked about their evening routine?
"I enjoy a warm bath, slip into cozy slippers, and immerse myself in a good book—a bedtime ritual that brings me joy."

● ● ●

Why did the wise senior citizen incorporate gratitude exercises into their daily routine?
They recognized that acknowledging blessings and cultivating gratitude shifts the focus to abundance and contentment.

●●●

What did the retired person say when asked about their morning routine?
"I savor a cup of tea, watch the sunrise, and welcome the day with open arms and a grateful heart."

●●●

Why did the elderly person have a regular exercise routine?
They understood that staying active keeps the body strong, the mind sharp, and the spirits high!

●●●

What did the wise retiree say about the importance of a morning routine?
"A well-structured morning routine sets the foundation for a successful, productive, and balanced day."

●●●

Why did the retiree always have a designated spot for their reading glasses?
They believed that a place for everything and everything in its place saves time and prevents unnecessary frustrations.

●●●

What did the grandparent say when asked about their evening routine?
"I unwind with a cup of herbal tea, engage in a relaxing hobby, and prepare for a peaceful night's sleep."

●●●

Why did the wise senior citizen enjoy a quiet moment of reflection before starting the day?
They believed in setting intentions, connecting with inner wisdom, and embracing the possibilities that lie ahead.

●●●

What did the retired person say when asked about their morning routine?
"I engage in gentle exercises, nourish my body with a healthy breakfast, and savor the moments of tranquility before the world wakes up."

●●●

SENIOR ADVENTURES

Why did the retired couple go skydiving? They wanted to prove that age is just a number, and they were determined to touch the sky in their golden years!

●●●

What did the adventurous senior say when asked about their latest travel escapade?
"I'm collecting passport stamps like they're souvenirs, and I'm not stopping until I've seen it all!"

●●●

Why did the wise senior citizen take up rock climbing?
They believed that reaching new heights was the perfect metaphor for conquering life's challenges and embracing adventure.

●●●

What did the retiree say when asked about their scuba diving experience?

"Exploring the underwater world is like entering a different dimension—it's a thrilling adventure that takes my breath away!"

●●●

Why did the grandparent decide to go on a cross-country road trip?

They wanted to create unforgettable memories, discover hidden gems, and prove that life is a never-ending journey.

●●●

What did the elderly person say when asked about their hot air balloon ride?

"Floating among the clouds, with the world below, I felt a sense of freedom and awe—a true adventure for the soul!"

●●●

Why did the wise retiree sign up for a salsa dance class?

They believed that dancing was the perfect way to stay active, express their joy, and spice up their retirement years!

●●●

What did the retired person say when asked about their hiking expedition?
"Nature's beauty was my reward, and the sense of accomplishment at the summit made every step of the adventure worthwhile!"

• • •

Why did the adventurous senior decide to learn how to surf?
They wanted to ride the waves of life, embrace the thrill of the ocean, and prove that age is just a wave in the journey.

• • •

What did the grandparent say when asked about their zip-lining experience?
"Soaring through the treetops, feeling the rush of adrenaline—it was an adventure that made me feel young at heart!"

• • •

Why did the wise senior citizen take up photography as a hobby?
They believed that through the lens, they could capture the beauty of the world and immortalize their own adventures.

• • •

What did the retiree say when asked about their camping trip?
"Sleeping under the stars, telling stories by the campfire—it was an adventure that reminded me of the simple joys in life."

●●●

Why did the adventurous senior decide to try their hand at painting?
They believed that art was a journey of self-expression, where each stroke was an adventure into their own creativity.

●●●

What did the elderly person say when asked about their kayaking adventure? "Paddling through the calm waters, surrounded by nature's serenity—I found peace, adventure, and a new sense of freedom."

●●●

Why did the wise retiree embark on a solo backpacking trip?
They wanted to challenge their limits, discover their inner strength, and prove that independence knows no age.

●●●

What did the retired person say when asked about their wildlife safari experience?

"Encountering majestic creatures in their natural habitat—a true adventure that made me appreciate the wonders of the animal kingdom."

●●●

Why did the adventurous senior decide to take up ballroom dancing?

They believed that gliding across the dance floor with a partner was like embarking on a graceful adventure of rhythm and connection.

●●●

What did the grandparent say when asked about their whitewater rafting excursion?

"Riding the rapids, feeling the rush of adrenaline—it was an adventure that washed away any concerns and brought pure exhilaration!"

●●●

Why did the wise senior citizen decide to try their hand at stand-up comedy?

They wanted to bring laughter to others, share their life experiences, and embark on a hilarious adventure of storytelling.

●●●

What did the retiree say when asked about their mountain biking adventure?
"Navigating rugged trails, feeling the wind in my hair—it was an adrenaline-fueled adventure that kept me young at heart!"

●●●

Why did the adventurous senior sign up for a cooking class?
They believed that exploring new flavors, mastering culinary skills, and delighting in food was a delicious adventure in itself.

●●●

What did the elderly person say when asked about their helicopter ride?
"Seeing the world from above, with a bird's-eye view—truly an adventure that gave me a fresh perspective on life!"

●●●

Why did the wise retiree decide to take up karate lessons?
They wanted to channel their inner strength, improve their balance, and embark on a martial arts adventure of self-discipline.

●●●

What did the retiree say when asked about their hot air balloon ride?
"Floating above the world, feeling the serenity of the skies—it was an adventure that made me appreciate the beauty of the Earth!"

● ● ●

Why did the adventurous senior sign up for a photography expedition?
They believed that capturing the world's beauty through the lens was an adventure that preserved memories and celebrated life's moments.

● ● ●

What did the elderly person say when asked about their hiking trip to the Grand Canyon?
"Descending into the depths, witnessing nature's masterpiece—it was an adventure that reminded me of the awe-inspiring grandeur of our planet!"

● ● ●

Why did the wise retiree decide to take up fishing?
They believed that casting a line, waiting patiently, and connecting with nature was an adventure that brought inner peace and reflection.

● ● ●

What did the retired person say when asked about their sailing expedition?

"Navigating the open waters, feeling the breeze against my face—it was an adventure that reminded me of the vastness of the world!"

●●●

Why did the grandparent decide to learn how to play a musical instrument?

They believed that music was a lifelong adventure, where every note played brought joy, harmony, and a sense of accomplishment.

●●●

What did the adventurous senior say when asked about their bungee jumping experience?

"Diving headfirst into the unknown, feeling the adrenaline rush—it was an adventure that taught me the thrill of taking a leap!"

●●●

Why did the wise senior citizen decide to try their hand at gardening?

They believed that nurturing plants, witnessing their growth, and creating a vibrant garden was an adventure of patience and beauty.

●●●

What did the retiree say when asked about their skiing adventure?
"Gliding down the slopes, feeling the crisp mountain air—it was an adrenaline-pumping adventure that made me feel alive!"

•••

Why did the adventurous senior sign up for a foreign language course?
They believed that learning a new language opened doors to different cultures, new connections, and exciting adventures abroad.

•••

What did the elderly person say when asked about their rock concert experience?
"Rocking out with the crowd, feeling the energy and music—it was an adventure that transported me to my youthful days!"

•••

Why did the wise retiree decide to take up birdwatching?
They believed that observing feathered friends in their natural habitats was an adventure that connected them with nature's wonders.

•••

What did the retired person say when asked about their motorhome road trip?
"Exploring new destinations, making spontaneous stops—it was an adventure that allowed me to bring my home on wheels!"

●●●

Why did the adventurous senior decide to try their hand at stand-up paddleboarding?
They believed that gliding on calm waters, surrounded by nature's beauty, was an adventure that brought them peace and serenity.

●●●

What did the grandparent say when asked about their horseback riding adventure?
"Riding through scenic trails, feeling the connection with my majestic companion—it was an adventure that reminded me of the freedom of the open road!"

●●●

Why did the wise senior citizen decide to take up astronomy as a hobby?
They believed that gazing at the stars, exploring the cosmos, and understanding the universe was an adventure that expanded their horizons.

●●●

LAUGHTER THERAPY

Why did the scarecrow become a comedian?
Because he was outstanding in his field of
jokes!

•••

Why did the scarecrow become a comedian?
Because he was outstanding in his field of
jokes!

•••

Why did the bicycle fall over?
Because it was two-tired!

•••

What do you call a bear that plays
the trumpet?
A tooty bear!

●●●

How do you make a lemon drop?
Just let it fall!

●●●

What do you call a fish wearing a crown?
King of the sea!

●●●

What did the ocean say to the shore?
Nothing, it just waved!

●●●

Why don't ants ever get sick?
Because they have little anty-bodies!

●●●

What do you call a bear that loves to dance?
The "bear-y" best dancer!

●●●

Why did the scarecrow take up gardening?
Because he wanted to grow corny jokes!

●●●

What do you call a bee that can't make up
its mind?
A maybee!

●●●

What do you call the wife of a hippie?
Mississippi.

●●●

Did you hear the watermelon joke?
It's pitiful.

●●●

How do you keep a bagel from
getting away?
Put lox on it.

●●●

How does the moon cut his hair?
Eclipse it.

●●●

What do lawyers wear to court?
Lawsuits

•••

Why do seagulls fly over the sea?
If they flew over the bay, they would be bagels.

•••

What do you call it when Batman skips church?
Christian Bale.

•••

How can you increase the heart rate of your 70-year-old husband?
Tell him you're pregnant.

•••

Where can single men over the age of 70 find younger women who are interested in them?
Try a bookstore under fiction.

•••

Why did the man get fired from the orange juice factory?
Lack of concentration.

•••

What was the radioactive older adult's superpower?
Gramma rays.

•••

What do you call an alligator in a vest?
An investigator.

•••

What do you call a camel with three humps?
Pregnant.

•••

Why did the coffee file a police report?
It got mugged.

•••

Why do birds fly south for the winter?
Because it's too far to walk.

•••

What do you call a can opener that
doesn't work?
A can't opener.

•••

What did the grape say when it got
stepped on?
Nothing, it just let out a little whine.

• • •

What did one toilet say to the other toilet?
You look flushed.

• • •

What do you call a sleeping bull?
A bulldozer!

• • •

What did the janitor say when he jumped
out of the closet?
"Supplies!"

• • •